BORN Wild in MONTANA

FARCOUNTRY PRESS

HELENA, MONTANA

Photography and text by Donald M. Jones

Right: With her twin cubs in tow, a grizzly sow moves through an alpine meadow.

Below: After momentarily losing sight of mom, two grizzly cubs stand on their hind legs to get a better view.

Title page: After a long romp with its siblings, a red fox kit naps at the entrance to its den.

Front cover: A fox kit takes a break from wrestling with its sibling to gaze at the photographer.

Back cover: This black bear cub isn't so sure dandelions make the best snack.

ISBN 10: 1-56037-487-X
ISBN 13: 978-1-56037-487-9

© 2009 by Farcountry Press
Photography © 2009 by Donald M. Jones

All rights reserved. This book may not be reproduced in whole or in part by any means (with the exception of short quotes for the purpose of review) without the permission of the publisher.

For more information about our books, write Farcountry Press, P.O. Box 5630, Helena, MT 59604; call (800) 821-3874; or visit www.farcountrypress.com.

Created, produced, and designed in the United States.
Printed in China.

13   12   11   10   09   1   2   3   4   5   6

*To Tess, the BEST mother
any two boys could ever wish for.*

Above: Unlike most owls, which perch high in trees, this juvenile short-eared owl prefers hiding amid spring grasses on the prairie.

Facing page: A shy black bear cub peeks out from behind a tree.

Introduction

As I look out the window, all I see is the thick blanket of snow that drapes across everything in my backyard in Troy, Montana. The winters are long here, and I yearn for the green grass and budding leaves of spring—the return of color and life to the landscape.

Even as winter has us in its grip, spring offers fleeting glimpses of what's to come. Most signs go unnoticed, but if you really look and listen, you just might spot a great horned owl readying a nest in February, or notice the disruption amongst the honking Canada geese as they discuss their nesting territories, or hear the familiar call of the black-capped chickadee as it searches for a mate.

For a photographer, spring is by far the most

exciting time of year. It's not so much a question of what and where to photograph, but rather how to photograph it all and not miss anything. Whether it's fox kits emerging from their den in the Bitterroot Valley, a ferruginous hawk nest on the Hi-Line, or burrowing owlets along the Missouri Breaks, new life is appearing everywhere.

As a wildlife photographer, I've determined that most of my subjects, if awake, are doing one of two things: eating or trying to avoid being eaten. With spring comes the arrival of youngsters, and that means a new set of activities: wonderment and play. Some of my most memorable moments as a wildlife photographer have been while sitting in a blind, observing a burrowing owlet watch in amazement as an ant crawls over its sibling's head, or watching a fox kit chase its brother's tail, only to realize that it, too, has a tail to chase.

Every spring I find myself growing antsy in March—teased by the mild weather, only to get a snowstorm that again enshrouds everything in white. By April there is no denying that spring has arrived, with red bison calves bounding and prancing on the prairie, processions of little yellow goslings paddling downstream, and downy great horned owlets peering out of their nest high in a cottonwood tree.

By early May, migrant birds begin to fill the woods with song as they stake out their nesting territories. Curious yet cautious, fox kits and badger kits start to emerge from their dens. In June, elk calves and deer fawns begin to appear, their wobbly attempts at walking quickly replaced by a more confident gait. Mountain goats and bighorn sheep teach their young to climb the rocky ridges they call home. Baby birds, with their insatiable appetites, keep their parents busy from sunrise to sunset.

This abundance of new life brings a bounty of photographic opportunities, often pulling me in five directions at once. How does one capture it all? The answer is time. It takes many springs, not just one. What I don't photograph this spring, perhaps I'll capture the following spring. It's a hard pill to swallow sometimes, but when I reflect back, I'm amazed by all I've seen, and I realize how incredible each of those Montana springs has been. It is an honor to be able to share these images of animals born free and *Born Wild in Montana.*

Above: A female northern goshawk listens as her mate calls, indicating he has food for their two downy chicks.

Facing page: With its mother feeding on succulent grasses close by, a cinnamon-colored black bear cub samples some budding willow leaves.

Right: Wet from a spring rain, a bighorn lamb rests at the edge of a meadow while its mother feeds nearby.

Facing page: Near a mountain lake in Glacier National Park, a cow moose greets her calf with a muzzle nuzzle. Moose calves can stand within hours of birth and are able to walk not long after.

Below: A female hooded merganser watches for danger as her chicks feed among the lily pads in a lake in northwestern Montana.

Above: This female ferruginous hawk stands guard over her brood in their large stick nest.

Left: A mountain goat kid finds comfort and warmth nestled against its mother.

Right: On a hillside of spring green, a cow elk affectionately touches noses with her spotted calf.

Below: Looking like a dandelion gone to seed, a burrowing owlet patiently awaits its mother's return with a meal of crickets or grasshoppers. Burrowing owls nest in burrows abandoned by mammals such as prairie dogs, badgers, and ground squirrels.

Above: This five-week-old red fox kit has crawled out of its cold, damp den to warm itself in the morning sun.

Left: A whitetail fawn uses its oversized ears like radar antennae to listen for predators.

Grizzly cubs receive most of their nourishment from their mothers' milk, not the alpine flowers this playful pair appears to be feeding on.

Right: While feeding with its mother alongside a roadway, this black bear cub appears surprised to see a photographer taking its picture.

Facing page: With its mother watching from a branch above, a baby porcupine practices its climbing skills on a Russian olive tree. Porcupines can climb trees at just one day old. They are born with soft quills that harden within an hour after birth.

Below: This baby hoary marmot sticks close to mom and keeps a watchful eye for predators, such as golden eagles. During the summer, hoary marmots fatten up on grasses, flowers, and herbs; they hibernate from September to June.

Left: Three coyote pups find this large crack in a boulder near their den to be the perfect place to play tag. Coyotes are born in early spring, and a typical litter has four to seven pups.

Below: A young golden-mantled ground squirrel handles a ripe dandelion like a band instrument before devouring it stem to flower.

Above: Waiting with mouths open wide, these young ravens call out to their mother for a meal. Ravens build their large nests on cliffs or in trees, constructing them of sticks and lining them with grass, bark, or colorful bits of string or cloth.

Right: Newly hatched northern harrier hawks huddle together in their ground nest in a prairie marsh. These tiny, helpless chicks will be able to fly in just thirty to thirty-five days.

Facing page: A tree swallow chick gazes out of the entrance to its nest in anticipation of its parents' return. Tree swallows build their nests inside tree holes abandoned by woodpeckers or other birds.

Above: Climbing to the highest point near its nest, this yellow-headed blackbird eagerly awaits a mouthful of scrumptious insects from its mother.

Right: A doe keeps her fawn squeaky clean; removing her fawn's scent is another way to keep it safe from predators.

Left: A northern hawk owlet in Glacier National Park calls out to its mother for a mousy morsel.

Facing page: This red fox kit appears to be giving its mother a good morning hug. Kits are born in March or April in litters of four to eight.

Below: This badger kit in southwestern Montana tests its teeth on a lichen-covered rock.

Above: Twin mountain goat kids make their way through alpine wildflowers along Glacier National Park's Logan Pass. Mountain goat nannies usually have twins; sure-footed and agile, mountain goat kids can climb steep cliffs shortly after birth.

Facing page: A black bear sow travels along a dandelion-covered slope, seemingly oblivious to the young hitchhiker on her back.

Above: A young yellow-pine chipmunk in the National Bison Range Wildlife Refuge holds its tail as if to say, "Does anyone have a comb?"

Facing page: This female swift fox wants to relax in the cool grass, but one of her kits has other ideas and is ready to play. Swift foxes are born in underground dens about three feet below the surface.

Above: When excited or nervous, pronghorns, such as this fawn, fluff up their rump hair. Pronghorns are North America's fastest land animal; at top speed, they can travel at more than fifty miles per hour.

Left: Burrowing owlet siblings spot a hawk flying high above. When in danger, owlets retreat to the safety of their underground burrows.

Above: An eared grebe at Benton Lake National Wildlife Refuge offers her chick a delicious lunch of aquatic insects—yum.

Above, top: This young beaver helps out around the lodge by gathering and storing food for the long winter.

Facing page: What could be more fun for a mountain goat kid than galloping over summer snow in Glacier National Park?

Above: Slow to emerge from their burrow, two Columbian ground squirrel siblings use caution before resuming their wrestling match.

Left: A baby desert cottontail comes out of its den on a cold April morning along the Missouri Breaks.

Facing page: This whitetail fawn shows off its namesake. Deer can travel at up to thirty miles per hour, and they wave their white tails like a flag as they run.

Above: A four-week-old elk calf high steps through wildflowers and grasses. Calves are covered in white spots to help camouflage them from predators; as they grow up, the spots disappear.

Facing page: Amid a field of glowing arrowleaf balsamroot, a bison calf enjoys a lazy May day.

Above: A coyote pup growls playfully at its patient parent. This naughty pup lives
in a den with its siblings and both parents, which share in the care of their young.

Facing page: Bison calves are born with red coats that eventually turn a rich, dark brown as
they mature. This calf will stay with its mother for about a year before setting off on its own.

Above: A whitetail fawn tests its legs in a sunlit meadow. White-tailed deer are one of two types of deer found in Montana; the other is the mule deer.

Right: With their tails twitching, these young black-tailed prairie dogs are ready to dart back to their burrow on their mother's command. Black-tailed prairie dogs live in large colonies on flat, open grasslands.

Facing page: This young pika proves that, as with humans, there is a clown in every family.

Above: With two rapidly growing chicks, the nest is getting a little crowded for this mother great horned owl in northwestern Montana.

Right: A mule deer mother reassures her fawn on a cool November day high in the Bitterroot Mountains. Mule deer have a gray coat in winter and a brown coat in summer.

Above, top and bottom: A mother Canada goose *(above, top)* shelters her eight goslings beneath her wings on a cool April morning, but then eventually allows them to investigate a pond *(above, bottom)* while under her watchful eye.

Facing page: Twin black bear cubs sporting beautiful white blazes on their chests bravely explore their surroundings.

Above, left: Knee deep in snow, this whitetail fawn will enjoy the company of its mother until spring, when it will begin to live on its own.

Above, right: A young mountain cottontail stands in the first of many snowfalls it will experience in its lifetime.

Facing page: A cow elk gently grooms her calf during a December squall.

Above: A young American robin sits motionless, hiding while it awaits its mother's return with breakfast; as usual, the menu is tasty worms.

Right: The three most important activities for a red fox kit: eating, sleeping, and plenty of playing.

Right: This baby great horned owl is having a hard time keeping its eyes open; for nocturnal owls, daylight means time to sleep.

Facing page: In order to evade predators on the Hi-Line prairie, a pronghorn fawn lies very still in the grass while its mother feeds nearby.

Below: While mom heads out to hunt ground squirrels, two badger kits stay close to their den entrance in anticipation of a tasty lunch.

Above: Black bears are excellent climbers, and this cub has found a nice spot to sit and gnaw on a fir branch while mom feeds below.

Left: Like a mini aircraft carrier, this mother loon carries her day-old chick on her back as she cruises through a lake in northwestern Montana.

Above, left and right: One at a time, please! A northern flicker returns with a meal for its hungry chicks, which greet their parent at the nest entrance with open mouths.

Facing page: An elk calf standing in frosted wild rose bushes strikes a pose.

Above: A six-month-old bighorn lamb sits huddled against a cold December breeze.

Right: This particular cinnamon-colored black bear seemed happy to carry all of her cubs on her back, like an opossum. The cubs played a game of "king of mom," pushing each other off until only one remained.

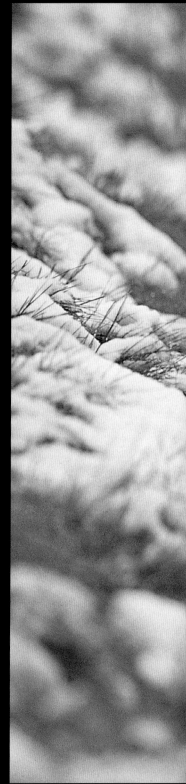

Above, left: Two baby Columbian ground squirrels find time to play in between munching on alpine flowers.

Above, right: A red fox kit emerges from its den with a big yawn.

Facing page: In the coming months, this gangly whitetail fawn will lose its spots and grow into those large ears and long legs.

Above: A whitetail fawn stretches its neck like a giraffe to get a better look at the photographer.

Right: This black bear cub scales a fallen log, only to be knocked off by its sibling waiting at the other end.

Above: A pronghorn buck stands next to a fawn in eastern Montana. A pronghorn's eyes sit far apart on its head so that it can see both forward and behind itself.

Right: As the sun sets on another day in Glacier National Park, a mountain goat kid nuzzles its mother.

Above: A coyote pup stands at attention in the rich spring grasses near its den site.

Facing page: This moose calf's light, chocolate-colored coat will turn a rich, dark brown as the summer wears on.

Above: The female calliope hummingbird does all the rearing of her young, with no help from the male. She has done well with her two babies, as they are about to outgrow their small, lichen-lined nest.

Facing page: A whitetail fawn appears to be whispering a secret to its sibling.

Right: This baby cedar waxwing has a bit more growing to do before it can leave the nest.

Above: A curious long-eared owlet peers from its nest as if to ask, "Whoooose there?"

Right: Bison typically only have one calf each year, but this cow on the National Bison Range Wildlife Refuge is lucky enough to have twins.

Left: A red-necked grebe chick finds security in riding on its mother's back for its first few weeks of life.

Right: Like children fighting for the last cookie, these comical burrowing owlets squabble over a grasshopper, a meal brought to them by their parents.

Below: This beaver kit hitches a ride on its mother's back as she collects food to store in their lodge.

Above: Like mother like daughter. This cub and sow are sporting matching white chest blazes, which is not uncommon among black bears.

Facing page: This black bear cub doesn't seem to care for the taste of dandelions, but most bears find them to be a tasty treat.

Right: A two-day-old Canada goose gosling explores a forest of grass at the edge of a pond.

Above: Like most baby animals, badgers love to roughhouse with their siblings. Short-legged and pigeon-toed, badgers won't break any land-speed records, but they are excellent diggers, using their long claws to excavate burrows and search for food.

Facing page: This coyote mother has her hands—or, in this case, her mouth—full as she attempts to carry her nine pups back into the den one at a time. Each time she places one in the den, another escapes.

Above: One day this fuzzy great gray owlet will have a wingspan of more than four feet. Great gray owls are the largest owl species in Montana.

Facing page: As a grizzly sow and her two cubs ascend a hillside green with sprouting grass, one of the cubs turns, as if to say good-bye.

About the photographer

One of the most respected wildlife photographers in the country, Donald M. Jones has spent the last twenty years viewing and photographing wildlife, from the Florida Everglades to the high Arctic—his real love, however, is for his home state of Montana. Jones's photographs have appeared in numerous periodicals, including *Audubon, Sierra, National Wildlife, Time, Field & Stream,* and *Outdoor Life.* His books include *Born Wild in Glacier National Park, Montana Wildlife Portfolio, Rocky Mountain Elk Portfolio,* and *Wings Over Montana.*

www.donaldmjones.com

Below: Standing tall and showing its white chest blaze, this black bear cub looks to be wearing a tuxedo.